LINDSEY
BAREHAM

THE LITTLE BOOK OF
BIG SOUPS

PENGUIN BOOKS

KT-197-513

PENGUIN BOOKS

Published by the Penguin Group. Penguin Books Ltd, 27 Wrights Lane, London
w8 5tz, England. Penguin Books USA Inc., 375 Hudson Street, New York,
New York 10014, USA. Penguin Books Australia Ltd, Ringwood, Victoria, Australia.
Penguin Books Canada Ltd, 10 Alcorn Avenue, Toronto, Ontario, Canada m4v 3b2.
Penguin Books (NZ) Ltd, 182–190 Wairau Road, Auckland 10, New Zealand · Penguin
Books Ltd, Registered Offices: Harmondsworth, Middlesex, England · This
selection is from *A Celebration of Soup* and *Onions without Tears*, by Lindsey Bareham,
first published by Michael Joseph 1993 and 1995. Published in Penguin Books 1994
and 1996. This edition published 1996. Copyright © Lindsey Bareham 1993, 1995.
All rights reserved · The moral right of the author has been asserted · Typeset by
Rowland Phototypesetting Ltd, Bury St Edmunds, Suffolk. Printed in England by
Clays Ltd, St Ives plc · Except in the United States of America, this book is sold
subject to the condition that it shall not, by way of trade or otherwise, be lent,
re-sold, hired out, or otherwise circulated without the publisher's prior consent in any
form of binding or cover other than that in which it is published and without a similar condition including this condition being imposed on the subsequent
purchaser · 10 9 8 7 6 5 4 3 2 1

CONTENTS

Clear Soups

Cold Soups

Introduction

Soup is one of man's oldest foods, and it is easy to see why it has survived the ages. Soup can be made from virtually anything at any season, and it can come in so many forms. A steaming bowl of heart-warming broth, a thick vegetable purée, an intensely flavoured consommé, or a meal in itself. It can be hot or cold, or somewhere in between, and it can be simple, elaborate, comforting or exotic. It can be perfectly plain or embellished with contrasting flavours.

I love the versatility of soup, and part of the fun is the complementary trimmings that can make a soup a super-soup: a sprinkling of fresh herbs, a few home-made croûtons, or the last-minute addition of a soft poached egg transforms an ordinary soup into something special.

In the 1990s, soup has made a dramatic comeback as a food of our times. It is healthy, fast to make and economical, providing an open-ended gastronomic journey that wends its way through the cuisines of the world.

For many people, stock remains the stumbling block to soup-making and whilst it is true that stock is often the body and soul of a soup, not all soups rely on it. Stock can be made from virtually any meat, fish, vegetable or herb, and different ingredients can be viewed as flavour building blocks. Two basic stock recipes are given; both can be stored in the fridge and freeze well.

Soup can be addictive, both making it and eating it. Surrender yourself; I promise you won't regret it.

CHICKEN STOCK

This is the stock I use all the time; it's an inevitable consequence of roast chicken.

MAKES ABOUT 1.75 LITRES (3 PINTS)

1 cooked chicken carcase, winglets, bones, giblets and
*   any skin, meat and jelly*
1 unpeeled onion, quartered
green part of 4 leeks, chopped
2 carrots, chopped
1 garlic clove, crushed with the flat of a knife
1 bay leaf
a small bunch of parsley
2 branches of thyme
6 peppercorns
a generous pinch of salt
about 2 litres (3½ pts) cold water

Put all the ingredients in a large pan, cover with the water and bring the water slowly to the boil. Turn down the heat and let the stock simmer gently, uncovered, for 2 hours.

Strain the stock into a bowl, let it cool and then refrigerate it. Remove the layer of fat that forms on the surface before using the stock. To concentrate the flavour, reduce the chilled stock by one-third.

FISH STOCK

Most of the goodness and flavour in fish stock comes from the bones and trimmings of fish. Fish heads are particularly good. All white fish and most crustaceans make satisfactory fish stocks, but avoid oily fish, such as mackerel, herring, sprat and sardine. Shrimp and prawn heads and tails give a surprising amount of flavour.

Because fish stocks cook quickly, any flavouring vegetables must be finely chopped. Onion, carrot, leek and fennel bulb, with parsley, thyme and half a bay leaf, are the usual choice.

Fish stock is never as clear as meat and vegetable stocks and shouldn't be clarified. The flavour of fish stock will deteriorate if you cook it for longer than specified: once you have strained it, you can strengthen its flavour by reduction in the normal way, if necessary.

MAKES ABOUT 1.1 LITRES (2 PINTS)

500–750g (1–1½ lb) bones, heads, tails and
    trimmings from non-oily fish
1 onion or leek, finely chopped
1 carrot, chopped
a bouquet garni made with a small bunch of parsley,
    a layer of fennel and a branch of thyme
4 peppercorns
a pinch of salt
about 1.5 litres (2½ pts) cold water

Rinse the bones, etc., under cold running water, carefully removing gills, blood and viscera. Chop the bones into 5 cm (2 inch) pieces. Pack all the ingredients in a stock-pot and cover with the water. Bring the water slowly to the boil, turn down the heat and let the stock simmer for 20 minutes, skimming any grey bubbles that rise to the surface. Strain the stock.

Quick Soups

COURGETTE SOUP WITH PARSLEY
AND BASIL

A pretty pale green cream soup flecked with dark green herbs
and enriched with eggs and Parmesan. Serve it with extra
Parmesan and plenty of crusty bread and butter.

SERVES 6

2 tbsp olive oil
1 large onion, finely chopped
6 medium courgettes, grated
salt and pepper
1.1 litres / 2 pts light chicken stock
2 tbsp flat-leaf parsley, finely chopped
2 tbsp basil, finely chopped
2 eggs
4 tbsp Parmesan, freshly grated

Using a pan that can hold the finished soup, heat the olive oil.
Sauté the onion until it is soft but not browned and stir in the
courgettes, ½ tsp of salt and a little pepper. Cover and sweat,
stirring a couple of times, for 5 minutes. Add the stock, bring
quickly to the boil and simmer for 10 minutes. Liquidize, and
return the soup to a clean pan. Beat the herbs into the eggs
and stir in the Parmesan. Bring the soup up to a simmer,

remove from the heat, and beat in the herb, egg and cheese mixture. Taste for seasoning and serve.

CREAM OF POTATO, LEEK AND ONION WITH BUTTERED ONIONS

This is the soup I make the most often and which never fails to please. It's made with the winning combination of leek, potato and onion, and here they are gently stewed in butter then cooked in water. The whole is liquidized into a silky creamy purée. Buttery strands of soft onion are stirred into the soup just before it's finished with a swirl of hot cream and a few snipped chives.

SERVES 4

2 large onions
50 g/2 oz butter
1 large leek, split and diced
450 g/1 lb floury potatoes, peeled and chopped
small bunch of parsley
salt and pepper
1.1 litres/2 pts water plus 1 chicken stock cube
100 ml/4 fl oz single cream
1 tbsp chopped chives

Chop one of the onions and put it in a medium saucepan with half the butter, the leek, the potatoes and the small bunch of 7 parsley. Season generously with salt and pepper, cover the pan and stew gently for 10 minutes, giving the pan the occasional stir. Cover the vegetables with the water in which the stock cube has been dissolved, and quickly bring the liquid to the boil. Cook at a vigorous simmer for approximately 15 minutes or until the vegetables are tender. Liquidize the soup and pour it through a sieve into a clean pan. Reheat and adjust the seasoning.

While the vegetables are cooking, halve the remaining onion through its root and slice it very finely. Heat the remaining butter in a small pan and gently soften the onion until it's floppy and golden; this will take at least 15 minutes. Tip the contents of the pan into the liquidized soup and simmer very gently for 5 minutes. Just before serving, bring the cream to boiling point and pour it in a pattern on top of the soup. Serve garnished with chives.

FENNEL AND TOMATO FISH SOUP WITH CHEAT'S ROUILLE

This soup, unlike bouillabaisse, which it resembles, can be made with any firm-textured fish and is all the better for being made with a mixture. To make this soup into a complete meal, increase the quantities of fish or add mussels. Oily fish, such as herring, mackerel, sardine and tuna, aren't suitable.

8   The Tabasco-spiked rouille, stirred into the soup or spread

on the croûtons and sprinkled with Gruyère, is the traditional way of livening up the flavours.

SERVES 4

2 tbsp olive oil
1 large onion, finely chopped
2 cloves of garlic, crushed
1 fennel bulb, finely chopped
225 g/8 oz tomatoes, peeled and chopped
5 cm/2 in piece of orange peel
salt and pepper
1.1 litres/2 pts fish stock
generous pinch of saffron strands
450 g/1 lb fish fillets, cut into 5 cm/2 in pieces

For the rouille:

200 g/7 oz canned or bottled pimientos, drained
1 large clove of garlic
1 tbsp olive oil
generous pinch of salt
about 6 drops of Tabasco sauce

Heat the olive oil and gently sauté the onion and garlic without letting them brown. Add the fennel and sweat for 5 minutes before adding the tomatoes, the orange peel, ¼ tsp of salt and a generous grinding of pepper. Let the vegetables simmer gently for 5 minutes or so until almost soft and pour on the heated stock. Bring to the boil and reduce slightly while you

9

steep the saffron in a little of the hot stock. Pour the saffron mixture into the soup, bring up to the boil and slip in the fish. Taste for seasoning and cook quickly for a couple of minutes.

Make the rouille by liquidizing all the ingredients together.

Serve in heated bowls with croûtons, grated Gruyère and the rouille separately.

GREEN FISH SOUP

Many soups are liquid versions of favourite combinations of foods. Here broccoli and white fish are puréed in a fennel-flavoured fish stock and enriched with cream; a wonderful and unusual-looking soup I learnt from Marion Jones of the Croque-en-Bouche at Malvern Wells.

SERVES 8

½ a large onion, thinly sliced
1 small leek, thinly sliced
25 g/1 oz unsalted butter
25 g/1 oz flour
1 litre/1¾ pts hot fish stock, flavoured with fennel and
  a grating of nutmeg
salt and pepper
450 g/1 lb skinned and filleted haddock, whiting, hake
  or conger eel, cut into chunks
350 g/12 oz sprouting broccoli or calabrese
150 ml/¼ pt double cream

Sweat the onion and leek in the butter until soft without letting it brown. Off the heat stir in the flour and cook again gently for a few minutes, stirring all the while. Remove from the heat again and stir in most of the stock. Bring to a simmer and cook for 10 minutes, taste for seasoning, and add the fish. Cook for 1 minute and allow to cool slightly before processing, blending at top speed or sieving until smooth.

Meanwhile, peel the broccoli or calabrese stalks, cut off some of the florets for a final garnish, and chop the rest. Cook the chopped part in just enough lightly salted water to cover. Drain, keeping the liquor, and refresh under cold water. Mix with some of the liquor and sieve into the fish soup, blending again if necessary. Dilute to taste with the remaining fish stock and broccoli liquor. Reheat until just below boiling point, add the cream, check the seasoning and serve garnished with the steamed broccoli florets.

MEADOW HERB SOUP WITH COURGETTES AND PEAS

A compote of new-season summer vegetables in a herby broth thickened with egg yolk, lemon juice and cream.

SERVES 4

25 g/1 oz butter
2 bunches spring onions, cut on the slant into 0.5 cm/
    ¼ in slices

225 g/8 oz peas, shelled weight
1 courgette, split and diced
salt and pepper
900 ml/1½ pts chicken stock
2 handfuls young spinach, rolled and sliced
leaves from a large bunch of watercress, chopped
1 small lettuce, finely shredded
2 egg yolks
1 tbsp lemon juice
2 tbsp double cream
1 tbsp each of chopped mint, chervil and chives

Melt the butter in a pan and stir in the spring onions. Cook for 5 minutes before adding the peas and courgette. Season with salt and pepper, cover the pan and sweat, stirring a couple of times, for 5 minutes. Add the stock, bring it quickly to the boil and simmer for 5 minutes before adding the spinach, watercress and lettuce. Mix together the egg yolks, lemon juice, double cream, mint, chervil and chives. Stir the mixture into the soup and cook without boiling for a couple of minutes.

MUSSELS AND SAFFRON WINE SOUP

This soup, which is known as Billi Bi, is a quick, easy but rich and luxurious variation on moules marinière. It should be a rich, velvety, pale yellow soup, thick with plump mussels – a meal in itself.

50 g / 2 oz butter
2 large shallots, finely chopped
400 ml / ¾ pt dry white wine
1 kg / 1 ¾ pts mussels, scrubbed and washed in several
changes of water
400 ml / ¾ pt good fish stock
½ tsp saffron threads
2 egg yolks, mixed with 150 ml / ¼ pt double cream
salt and pepper
2 tbsp flat-leaf parsley, chopped

Melt the butter and soften the shallots. Pour on the wine and let it bubble up before adding the mussels. Cover and cook over a fierce heat, shaking the pan a few times, until the mussels open. Place a colander over a bowl and tip on the mussels. Remove the mussels from their shells and set aside (chuck out the shells).

Strain the liquid into a pan, add the fish stock and bring up to a simmer. Stir in the saffron, remove from the heat and carefully whisk in the egg and cream liaison. Return to the heat, warm the soup through without boiling and add the mussels. When the soup has thickened, taste for seasoning. Pour into warmed bowls, sprinkle on the parsley and serve with plenty of crusty bread for dunking.

PAPPA AL POMODORO

A traditional peasant soup from Tuscany, made with yesterday's bread and tomatoes from the garden. It relies on ripe tomatoes that are full of flavour, and it's worth using really good olive oil for the garnish. It can be eaten hot, warm or cold.

SERVES 4–6

4–5 tbsp olive oil
3 cloves of garlic, crushed and chopped
750 g/1½ lb very ripe tomatoes, peeled and cut into
  chunks
10 basil leaves, shredded
1 litre/1¾ pts chicken stock
salt and pepper
1 very stale good white or wholemeal loaf, weighing
  about 450 g/1 lb, crust removed
freshly grated Parmesan

Heat the olive oil and sauté the garlic for a minute without browning. Add the tomatoes and basil and let the ingredients bubble for 5 minutes. Pour on the stock, season with salt and pepper and, when the soup is boiling, stir in the bread, crust removed, sliced and torn into small pieces. Cook for a few minutes until the bread flops and merges in with the tomatoes. Turn off the heat, cover and leave to stand for one hour.

Stir the soup well, check the seasoning and serve each helping with a slosh of olive oil and grated Parmesan cheese.

PEA SOUP WITH PARMESAN CROÛTES

An intriguing seventeenth-century *zuppa di piselli* which is served over bread fried in olive oil and dredged with grated Parmesan cheese.

SERVES 6

700 g / 1½ lb fresh or good-quality frozen peas
1 large onion, finely chopped
2–3 large cloves of garlic, chopped
1.3 litres / 2¼ pts good chicken stock
25 g / 1 oz toasted pine nuts
15 g / ½ oz sugar
juice of 1 lemon
salt and freshly ground white pepper

For the croûtes:

6 slices fine-grain brown bread
approx. 6 tbsp olive oil
approx. 50 g / 2 oz Parmesan, freshly grated

Cook the peas with the onion and garlic in the stock for 15 minutes, and purée. Meanwhile, coarsely pound the pine nuts with the sugar and lemon juice. Mix into the soup and taste for seasoning.

To serve the soup, fry the slices of bread in the olive oil until they are crisp and brown on both sides. Place a slice of the bread in the bottom of each heated serving bowl and sprinkle liberally with Parmesan. Reheat the soup and pour it over the bread. Serve with more freshly grated Parmesan.

WHITE BEAN SOUP

This is a store-cupboard version of a classic Italian soup. If possible, add a rasher or two of bacon with the onion, and a generous pinch of thyme, rosemary or mixed herbs. The flavours will develop and improve if the soup is left overnight, but in this case you may need to add a little more liquid.

SERVES 4

1 scant dsp olive oil
1 medium onion, finely diced
2 fat cloves of garlic, chopped
2 × 400 g/14 oz cans white beans, rinsed
900 g/1½ pts chicken stock or equivalent using stock cubes
salt and pepper
2 tbsp parsley, finely chopped
1 peperoni sausage, finely sliced
juice of ½ small lemon

Heat the oil and gently sauté the onion until soft but not brown. Add the garlic and the drained beans and stir around before adding the stock. Bring to the boil, season generously, and liquidize half the soup. Return to the pan, stir in the parsley, peperoni, and lemon juice. Simmer for 3 minutes and serve with croûtons, sprinkled with a few drops of Tabasco sauce. This soup is also very good eaten with a spoonful of bottled pesto sauce and a splosh of olive oil.

WILD MUSHROOM SOUP

You can use any mushrooms for this elegant velvety soup; the important thing is to use plenty of them. The secret of its distinctive haunting flavour is nutmeg and lemon juice.

SERVES 4

50 g/2 oz stale brown bread, crust removed
2–3 tbsp milk
50 g/2 oz butter
700 g/1½ lb mixed mushrooms, chopped
1 medium garlic clove, finely chopped
1 tbsp parsley, finely chopped
nutmeg, salt and pepper
570 ml/1 pt chicken stock
juice of ½ small lemon
100 ml/4 fl oz double cream

Moisten the bread with the milk and leave to soak. Melt the butter, stir in the mushrooms, adding the garlic and parsley, and cook them gently for 5 minutes, stirring occasionally. Season generously with freshly grated nutmeg, salt and pepper, and add the chicken stock. Bring to the boil, turn down the heat immediately, cover and simmer gently for 10 minutes.

Liquidize, return to the pan, adjust the seasoning with nutmeg, salt, pepper and lemon juice and bring back to the boil. Stir in the cream and serve.

Thick Soups and Whole Meal Soups

BLACK BEAN SOUP WITH TOMATO SALSA

This is a Caribbean recipe, from Cuba. The cayenne and garlic give the soup a kick which is echoed in the *salsa*. It is a lovely mix of textures too.

SERVES 4−6

2 tbsp oil
1 medium onion, chopped
2 fat cloves of garlic, peeled and crushed
1 stick of celery with leaves, chopped
225 g/8 oz black beans, soaked overnight in cold water
2.3 litres/3 pts vegetable stock or water
2 tsp salt
¼ tsp black pepper
½ tsp cayenne pepper
juice of 1 large lemon
3 tbsp dry sherry
freshly grated Cheddar

For the salsa:

1 tbsp brown sugar
1 tsp salt
1 tbsp lemon juice
8 drops of Tabasco sauce

1 cm/½ in piece of fresh ginger, peeled
2 cloves of garlic, peeled
450 g/1 lb very ripe tomatoes, peeled, cored and
    chopped

Heat the oil in a large pan. Soften the onion, then add the garlic and celery, stirring frequently. Mix in the drained beans and pour in the stock or water. Bring to the boil, lower the heat, cover the pan and simmer gently for about 2 hours, until the beans are soft. Use a slotted spoon to fish out about half the beans. Blend them to a purée with some of the hot stock. Stir the purée back into the soup, season with the salt and the two peppers, and simmer for 10 minutes, stirring constantly. Just before serving stir in the lemon juice and sherry.

To make the *salsa*, dissolve the sugar and salt in the lemon juice and stir in the Tabasco sauce. Pound the ginger and garlic to make a paste, stir into the lemon juice mixture and mix thoroughly with the tomatoes.

Serve with a covering of freshly grated Cheddar, and hand the tomato *salsa* separately. This soup is also delicious garnished with chopped hard-boiled eggs and savory or celery leaves.

CABBAGE AND BACON SOUP

This is a chunky soup which can be turned into a complete meal by adding dumplings or by serving it with bread and a slab of Cheddar. Alternatively, it can be liquidized to make a thick rib-sticker that goes well with crunchy croûtons.

SERVES 4

25 g/1 oz butter
1 medium onion, chopped
100 g/4 oz smoked bacon, rinds removed and diced
1 medium potato, peeled and diced
900 ml/1½ pts chicken stock
salt and pepper
450 g/1 lb Savoy cabbage, cored and shredded
3 tbsp single cream (optional)

Melt the butter and soften the onion with the bacon, cooking until the onion is limp and the bacon is beginning to crisp. Stir in the diced potato, stirring around so everything is nicely mixed up. Cook for a couple of minutes before pouring on the stock. Season lightly with salt and generously with pepper. Bring to the boil and cook vigorously for 10 minutes before adding the cabbage. Cook for a further 5 minutes or until the cabbage is tender. Serve immediately. If you have liquidized the soup, return it to a clean pan, reheat and adjust the seasoning. Serve with a swirl of cream and croûtons.

CALDILLO DE PESCADO

This is a typically robustly flavoured Spanish fish soup. Serve it with plenty of crusty bread.

SERVES 6–8

1.4 kg/3 lb skinned, filleted cod, cut into big pieces
salt and pepper
50 ml/2 fl oz lemon juice
50 ml/2 fl oz olive oil
2 medium onions, finely chopped
1 fresh red or green chilli pepper, finely chopped
1 red pepper, de-seeded and diced
2 cloves of garlic, crushed
900 g/2 lb small new or waxy-variety potatoes, sliced
*   wafer thin and rinsed*
½ tsp oregano or 1 tsp chopped fresh marjoram
275 ml/½ pt dry white wine
1.1 litres/2 pts fish stock
fresh chopped herbs to garnish

Season the pieces of cod with salt and pepper and sprinkle with the lemon juice. Heat the oil and gently fry the onions, chilli and red pepper until soft. Add the garlic, the cod, and after a couple of minutes pile in the potatoes. Sprinkle on the herbs and pour on the wine and fish stock. Bring quickly to the boil, turn down to a simmer, and cook, covered, for 15 minutes or until the potatoes are cooked. Serve sprinkled with the garnishing herbs.

CHICKPEA SOUP WITH FRIED EGGS

A simple, surprising and delicious soup.

SERVES 6

225 g/8 oz chickpeas, soaked overnight in cold water
4 tbsp olive oil
1 medium onion, finely chopped
2 cloves of garlic, finely chopped
1 tbsp mint leaves, finely chopped
700 ml/1¼ pts chicken stock
salt and pepper
juice of ½ a lemon
6 eggs

Cover the chickpeas with fresh water, bring slowly to the boil, then simmer gently for at least 1 hour until quite soft. Drain, reserving 275 ml/½ pt of the cooking liquid. Heat 2 tbsp of the olive oil and soften the onion and garlic. Transfer to a blender or food processor, add the mint leaves and 150 ml/¼ pt of the stock, and purée. Add the chickpeas with the reserved 275 ml/½ pt of cooking liquid, and purée. Return to a clean pan, add the rest of the stock and simmer for 5 minutes, stirring well. Taste and season with salt, pepper and lemon juice. Just before serving, heat the rest of the olive oil and fry the eggs. Pour the soup into bowls, and slip a fried egg into each bowl.

Provide good bread for dunking and mopping.

CREAM OF FENNEL SOUP

This is a luxurious soup, with a high proportion of fennel to liquid and much fortification from cream, butter, white wine, and Pernod.

SERVES 6

110 g/4 oz butter
2 onions, chopped
4 large fennel bulbs, coarsely chopped
1 glass of dry white wine
1 tsp fennel seeds
900 ml/1½ pts light chicken stock
large measure of Pernod
275 ml/½ pt whipping cream
salt and pepper

Melt the butter and sweat the onions and fennel over a very low heat, covered, until thoroughly wilted and soft. Stir occasionally: this will take about 30 minutes but the longer and slower, the better. Add the white wine and fennel seeds and simmer gently, uncovered, for 10 minutes. Add the chicken stock and simmer, covered, for a further 30 minutes. Liquidize and pass through a fine sieve into a clean pan.

In a small pan, heat the Pernod and ignite. When the flames subside, stir into the soup, followed by the cream. Reheat but don't allow to boil. Taste and correct the seasoning with salt and pepper. Serve.

EGG BOUILLABAISSE WITH PEAS

Bouillabaisse, the saffron-coloured fisherman's soup of the south of France, gets its name from a style of cooking – *bouillon-abaisse*, meaning rapidly boiled to reduce. In this version, peas and eggs replace the fish.

SERVES 6

6 tbsp olive oil
2 leeks, or 6 spring onions, and 1 small onion, sliced
2 large ripe tomatoes, peeled, cored and chopped
6 new potatoes, scraped and sliced
5 cloves of garlic, peeled, halved and crushed
1 fennel bulb, sliced
5 cm / 2 in piece of dried orange peel
large pinch of saffron strands
1.4 litres / 2½ pts chicken stock or water
450 g / 1 lb shelled peas, or frozen petits pois
salt and pepper
1 egg per person

1 tbsp parsley, chopped
6 slices oven-dried French bread

For maximum ease of cooking and serving you need a large, low ovenproof dish for bouillabaisse. Heat the oil and lightly sauté the leeks or onion and spring onions. Add the tomatoes, potatoes, garlic, fennel, orange peel and saffron, stirring everything together thoroughly. Turn up the heat as high as possible and add the boiling stock or water, the peas, ½ tsp salt and several grinds of black pepper. Boil hard for about 10 minutes, or until the potatoes are almost cooked. Turn down the heat and poach the eggs in the soup (you may find it easier to poach the eggs separately, slipping them into the tureen or individual bowls at the last moment). Sprinkle lavishly with chopped parsley. The soup is served over a slice or two of oven-dried bread.

EGYPTIAN LENTIL SOUP

Onion and garlic give a mellow flavour to this thick lentil soup that is seasoned first with cumin and later by lemon juice and a generous garnish of crispy fried onion with garlic and fresh parsley or coriander.

SERVES 8

2 large onions, chopped
4 garlic cloves, crushed
2 tbsp olive oil

2 tsp ground cumin
450 g/1 lb red lentils, washed
1 bay leaf
½ tsp dried oregano
salt and pepper
2.3 litres/4 pts stock or water

For the garnish:

1½ large onions, chopped
4 tbsp vegetable oil
3 garlic cloves, minced
1 tsp ground coriander
4 tbsp flat-leaf parsley or fresh coriander, finely chopped
pitta bread
lemon wedges

In a large saucepan sauté the onion and garlic in the olive oil for about 5 minutes, letting the onion brown slightly. Stir in the cumin, letting it cook briefly before adding the lentils, bay leaf and oregano, salt and pepper and then the stock. Bring to the boil and simmer for about 40 minutes until the lentils are tender. Meanwhile prepare the garnish by frying the onion in the oil until it is very brown. Add the garlic and ground coriander and cook for 2 more minutes.

When the lentils are ready, remove the bay leaf and liquidize the soup. Taste and adjust the seasoning. Serve the soup with a garnish of spiced onions, a sprinkling of parsley or fresh coriander, triangles of toasted pitta bread and lemon wedges.   27

FRENCH ONION SOUP

It's the long, slow cooking of the onions to bring out their sweet, rich flavour which makes this soup so special. Of all the onion soups this one is most worth making 24 hours in advance to allow the flavours to develop.

SERVES 6–8

75 g/3 oz butter
1.8 kg/4 lb large onions, halved through the core then
    very finely sliced
½ tsp sugar
1 heaped tbsp flour
1 wineglass (approx. 150 ml/¼ pt) dry white wine or cider
    2 litres/3½ pts stock, the richer the better, but water
    or water and stock will also be good
salt and pepper
3 tbsp brandy

Melt the butter in a large, heavy-bottomed, lidded pan. Stir in the onions, cover, and sweat very gently, stirring every now and again, for 15 minutes. Uncover, turn up the heat slightly, sprinkle in the sugar and cook for at least 45 minutes, stirring regularly, until the onions are tender and a deep golden brown. Sprinkle over the flour, then stir and pour on the white wine or cider. Let it bubble up and have ready the boiling stock or water and stock. Pour it over the onions, bring the soup back to the boil, then simmer, uncovered, for 40 minutes. Correct the seasoning with plenty of salt and pepper.

Just before serving, stir in the brandy. Serve with cheese croûtes, made by buttering 2 thick slices of French bread per person and then baking them until hard and golden. Rub the slices with cut garlic, sprinkle with grated Gruyère or Parmesan, and brown under a hot grill.

JERUSALEM ARTICHOKE SOUP

Depending on the age of the artichokes, this soup can be very thick. The optional milk, or milk and cream, is used to thin the soup as well as making it creamier. Small, young artichokes need only be scrubbed: bigger ones need peeling, and there is inevitable wastage. Once peeled, drop them into acidulated water (a dash of lemon juice or vinegar) as they discolour instantly.

SERVES 6

110 g / 4 oz butter
1 large onion, chopped
1 clove of garlic, chopped
900 g / 2 lb Jerusalem artichokes, peeled and chopped
½ a stick of celery, chopped
salt and pepper
1.1 litres / 2 pts light chicken or turkey stock, or water
up to 275 ml / ½ pt milk, or half-milk and half double
  cream (optional)

Heat half the butter in a large pan and soften the onion, then stir in the garlic, artichokes and celery. Season with ½ tsp of salt, cover, and leave to sweat for a couple of minutes. Pour on the stock, bring to the boil, turn down to a simmer, cover partially, and leave to cook until all the vegetables are soft. Purée, then return to a clean pan and add the milk or milk and cream mixture if using. Bring to a simmer, taste and season, adding more liquid if the soup is too thick. Whisk in the last of the butter.

Serve scattered with crisply fried bacon pieces, or with croûtons made by rolling diced white bread in olive oil, then baking at 400°F/200°C/Gas Mark 6 for 10 minutes until crisp and golden.

POTATO AND WATERCRESS SOUP

Take a potato and an onion, and you have the basis for countless different soups. This is one way of doing it, here 'garnished' and seasoned with the peppery tang of raw watercress and the sweet acidity of tomatoes.

SERVES 4–6

900 g/2 lb potatoes, peeled, diced and rinsed
2 onions, chopped
1.1 litres/2 pts water
salt, pepper and nutmeg or mace to taste
275 ml/½ pt milk
4 large tomatoes, peeled, quartered, seeded and cored

leaves of 2 bunches of watercress, finely chopped
dash of white wine or lemon juice

Boil the potatoes and onions in the salted water until soft. Purée by pressing the soup through a sieve, return to the heat, and add the milk, plenty of pepper and a scraping of nutmeg or mace. Taste and adjust the seasoning. Reheat.

Dice the tomatoes. When ready to serve, stir in the chopped watercress leaves, the diced tomato, and the wine or lemon juice.

POTÉE LORRAINE

The perfect winter warmer, otherwise known as pork and beans or boiled ham with vegetables. It's a substantial meal and the recipe should be used as a guideline. For example, the sausages can be omitted and if broad beans aren't available, double the quantity of green beans (frozen are fine).

SERVES 6

1 tbsp lard
2 onions, sliced
4 leeks, sliced
450 g/1 lb ham hock
1.75 litres/3 pts water
4 large carrots, peeled and chopped
2 small turnips, chopped

110 g/4 oz haricot beans, soaked overnight
2 cloves
1 bay-leaf
4 cloves of garlic, crushed
225 g/8 oz piece lean smoked bacon
4 sprigs celery leaves
6 pure pork sausages
6 medium potatoes, peeled, halved and rinsed
200 g/7 oz green beans, trimmed
200 g/7 oz broad beans, shelled weight
200 g/7 oz peas, shelled weight
½ small Savoy cabbage, shredded
salt and pepper
nutmeg

Melt the lard in a huge pan, gently soften the onions, then stir in the leeks. Lay the ham hock over the vegetables and cover with the water. Bring to the boil, skim, turn down the heat and simmer for 1 hour.

Add the carrots, turnips, haricot beans, cloves, bay-leaf, garlic, bacon and celery leaves. Bring back to a simmer and cook for 90 minutes before adding the sausages and potatoes. Re-establish a simmer and cook for a further 30 minutes. Ten minutes before the end of cooking, turn up the heat, add the green beans, broad beans, peas and cabbage, and more water if necessary, and cook at a brisk boil. Taste to see if the stew needs salt, and add plenty of pepper and a generous seasoning of nutmeg.

Slice the meat and serve with the sausages, vegetables and broth.

ROASTED ONION AND TOMATO SOUP WITH GREEN DUMPLINGS

A gem of a soup: the vegetables are roasted then liquidized and used as a poaching broth for delectably light herb dumplings.

SERVES 4–6

For the soup:

3 Spanish onions, halved through their middles, roots trimmed but skins left on
900 g/2 lb plum tomatoes
4 big garlic cloves, cracked with a clenched fist but skins left on
2 carrots, split but unpeeled
900 ml/1½ pts vegetable or light chicken stock
salt and pepper

For the dumplings:

110 g/4 oz soft goat's cheese
50 g/2 oz fresh breadcrumbs
1 tbsp each of finely chopped chives, parsley, mint and basil or fresh coriander
salt and pepper
1 large egg, beaten

Pre-heat the oven to 400°F/200°C/Gas Mark 6. Place the onion halves cut side down on a heavy baking tray. Stand the tomatoes on their core end, and tuck the garlic and carrots around them. Bake for 40 minutes.

Meanwhile make the dumplings. Put the goat's cheese in a bowl and mash it well with a fork. Mix in the breadcrumbs and herbs and season with salt and pepper. Mix the beaten egg into the cheese mixture. Take a teaspoon of the mixture, and with a second teaspoon mould it into a little dumpling. Continue until all the mixture is used up.

When the vegetables are cooked, allow them to cool slightly and then remove their skins. Place them, and any juices, into the bowl of a food processor or blender and top up with the stock. Liquidize and pour the soup through a sieve into a saucepan. Heat the soup until it's simmering, adjust the seasoning with salt and pepper, and then add the dumplings. Poach for 3 to 4 minutes or until they're firm. Serve immediately.

SCALLOP AND POTATO CREAM
WITH CORAL

Scallops and potatoes are a marvellous combination in almost any form. This soup, made with a purée of potatoes, laced with chopped milk-poached scallops then garnished with slivers of bright orange coral, is a sort of liquid *coquilles St-Jacques*. It is easy and quick to make and unbelievably delicious.

50 g/2 oz butter
2 small shallots, finely chopped
450 g/1 lb potatoes, peeled and diced
salt and pepper
570 ml/1 pt hot fish stock
4 large cleaned scallops with their coral (total weight
  approx. 350 g/12 oz)
275 ml/½ pt milk
2 egg yolks
75 ml/3 fl oz double cream
1 tsp chives, snipped

Heat 40 g/1½ oz of the butter and soften the shallots. Stir in the potato, season with ½ tsp of salt and a few grinds of black pepper. Pour on the hot fish stock, stir, cover and simmer for 10 minutes. When the potatoes are soft, purée the contents of the pan. Pour and press through a fine sieve into a clean pan.

Meanwhile rinse the scallops and trim away any tough bits and the pinky/grey frilly gills. Cut off the coral and set aside. Dice the white meat and put it in a pan with the cold milk and a generous pinch of salt. Bring to a simmer and cook for a couple of minutes. Tip the chopped scallops and their cooking milk into the potato purée and whisk thoroughly. Bring back to a simmer, adjust the seasoning and remove the pan from the heat.

Beat the egg yolks into the cream, add a ladleful of the soup, then another, and stir the liaison into the pan. Return the pan to the heat and warm through without boiling. Just before serving, melt the remaining butter and gently sauté the scallop coral, either whole, halved or chopped.

Pour the soup into warmed bowls and garnish with the coral and a few snips of chives.

SHRIMP SOUP

An exquisite, delicately flavoured soup, made with stock from the shrimp shells, thickened with breadcrumbs, and given a velvety finish with an egg and cream liaison.

SERVES 2–4

570 ml/1 pt cooked shrimps, pink or brown
225 g/8 oz bones, heads, tails and trimmings from
non-oily fish
1 small onion, chopped
2.5 cm/1 in piece of lemon peel
small bundle of herbs suitable for a fish stock (see
page 4)
900 ml/1½ pts water
3 tbsp white breadcrumbs
50 g/2 oz butter
juice of ½ a lemon
a pinch of freshly grated nutmeg
1 egg yolk

150 ml / ¼ pt double cream
salt and pepper
parsley or chervil

Shell the shrimps and put their shells, the fish bones et cetera, onion, lemon peel and herbs into a pan with the cold water. Bring to the boil and simmer for 20 minutes. Strain the liquid and stir in the breadcrumbs.

Meanwhile pound or blend the shrimps with the butter, adding the lemon juice and a pinch of nutmeg. Turn the purée into a pan and whisk in the shrimp stock thickened with the breadcrumbs. Simmer for 5 minutes and then press through a fine sieve into a clean pan. Beat the egg yolk with the cream, stir in a ladleful of the hot soup, and slowly whisk the liaison back into the pan. Taste for seasoning.

Pour into warmed bowls and garnish with a spray of chervil or a little chopped parsley.

Clear Soups

CHICKEN AND WATERCRESS SOY SOUP

This is a light, elegant Chinese soup that relies on decent chicken stock. It can also be made with Chinese leaves or sorrel and can be made more of by adding 3 or 4 shrimp balls per serving.

SERVES 4–6

1.1 litres/2 pts chicken-based stock
2 bunches of watercress, stems trimmed
175 g/6 oz raw chicken breast
2 tbsp light soy sauce
1 tsp sugar
4 spring onions, finely chopped

Bring the stock to simmering point. Blanch the watercress in a pan of boiling water for a few seconds. Refresh immediately in cold water to prevent further cooking. Slice the chicken into thin slices about 5 cm/2 in long, and blanch them in a little of the boiling stock for 2 minutes.

Add the blanched watercress and chicken to the stock, then add the soy sauce and the sugar. Bring back to a simmer, tip in the spring onions and serve with Chinese steamed buns.

FISH SOUP WITH CRAB AND MELON

A delicate, dainty summer appetizer.

SERVES 4

1.1 litres/2 pts fish stock
225 g/8 oz ripe and aromatic melon flesh
225 g/8 oz white crabmeat
4 thin slices of peeled lemon
salt and white pepper
1 dsp chervil or coriander leaves

Slowly reduce the fish stock by one-third while you scoop out the melon flesh with a melon-baller or cut it into equal-sized shapes. Divide the crabmeat and melon between four bowls, add a lemon slice and pour over the reduced fish stock. Check the seasoning, and serve garnished with chervil or coriander leaves.

PASTA IN BRODO CON FEGATINI E PISELLI

This is a lovely combination of fresh peas (frozen will do), short lengths of fine pasta, and quickly sautéed chicken liver. The quantities can be increased to make it more filling.

110 g / 4 oz fine pasta, broken into small pieces
1.75 litres / 3 pts chicken stock
350 g / 12 oz young peas, shelled weight or frozen
petits pois
40 g / 1½ oz butter
12 chicken livers, rinsed and chopped or sliced
Parmesan

Pre-cook bought pasta in boiling salted water according to the packet instructions. Drain and tip into the stock with the peas. Meanwhile heat the butter and seal the chicken liver pieces, stir-frying swiftly. Transfer to the soup with their butter. Grate over some Parmesan and serve with more.

STRACCIATELLA

Stracciatelle means 'little rags' and this is what this soup looks like. It's important to use decent stock; apart from that all the ingredients come from the store cupboard.

SERVES 4–6

3 eggs, beaten
4 tbsp Parmesan, freshly grated
4 tbsp fine fresh white breadcrumbs
finely grated zest of 1 lemon
1.4 litres / 2½ pts rich chicken stock

freshly grated nutmeg
salt and pepper

In a bowl, mix together the eggs, Parmesan, breadcrumbs and lemon zest with 225 ml/8 fl oz of the cold stock. Season generously with nutmeg, salt and pepper. Bring the remaining stock to the boil. Pour the egg mixture into the stock and stir quickly and thoroughly with a fork. Reduce the heat and simmer gently for 2 minutes, breaking up the eggs with a fork until they resemble little rags. Serve immediately with extra Parmesan.

Cold Soups

CHILLED BROAD BEAN SOUP
WITH SAVORY

A delicately flavoured, elegant and pretty pale green soup that
makes the most of young broad beans. Marjoram or celery
leaves could be used in place of savory.

SERVES 4

450 g/1 lb young broad beans, shelled weight
700 ml/1 pt chicken stock
1 tbsp savory, chopped finely
juice of ½ a lemon
salt and pepper
50 ml/2 fl oz double cream
50 ml/2 fl oz plain yoghurt
1 tbsp savory leaves

Reserve four broad beans and add the rest to the gently simmering stock. Cook gently for 5 minutes, purée, then sieve.
Stir in the chopped savory and the lemon juice, and adjust the
seasoning with salt and pepper. Chill the soup for 4 hours,
then garnish with the cream and yoghurt and decorate with
the fresh savory leaves and the reserved four beans, peeled and
chopped.

CHILLED DRIED APRICOT AND
LENTIL SOUP

This is a surprisingly delicious and very sustaining soup.

SERVES 6

225 g/8 oz brown or Puy lentils
110 g/4 oz dried apricots
1 tbsp olive oil
1 medium onion, finely chopped
2 cloves of garlic, chopped
1.1 litres/2 pts chicken stock
salt and pepper
lemon juice
½ tsp ground cardamom
150 ml/5 fl oz plain, good-quality yoghurt
1 tbsp each mint and coriander, chopped

Rinse the lentils, tip them into a pan and cover them with cold water. Bring to the boil, covered, over a moderate heat. Turn off the heat and leave for 60 minutes, then drain and transfer to a bowl. Meanwhile cover the apricots with warm water and leave to soak for 30 minutes. Drain and chop.

Heat the oil in a pan that can hold the entire soup. Gently cook the onion until limp but not browned, then stir in the garlic and sauté for a further 2 minutes. Add the lentils, apricots and stock, and season with a generous pinch of salt and several grinds from the peppermill. Stir in the cardamom, bring to the boil slowly, and simmer, covered, for 45 minutes or untilthe lentils are on the point of collapse. Purée, taste and adjust the seasoning with salt, pepper and lemon juice. Cool, stir in the yoghurt, chill. Check the seasoning again and serve garnished with the chopped mint and coriander.

CHILLED PASSION-FRUIT AND MELON SOUP

A Russian version of this delicate summer soup omits the passion-fruit and adds 150 ml/5 fl oz of soured cream, stirred in at the end.

SERVES 4

1 ripe melon, weighing approx. 900 g/2 lb
200 ml/7 fl oz dry white wine
5 passion-fruit, cut in half
50–100 g/2–4 oz sugar
400 ml/¾ pt water .
juice of 1 lime or lemon

Scoop out the pips of the melon, reserving some, and chop the flesh into pieces, discarding the skin. Purée the flesh with the wine and when smooth, add the flesh and pips scooped from the halved passion-fruit and process lightly. Pour into a bowl.

44 Meanwhile dissolve the sugar in the water over a low heat,

then simmer for a few minutes. Cool. Use the sugar, water and lime or lemon juice to season the soup, adding a little of each alternately until you end up with the right flavour. Chill.

Rinse the reserved pips, spread them out on a sheet of foil and toast under a slow grill. Serve separately as a garnish.

CURRIED APPLE SOUP

This surprising soup has a light and fluffy texture. The curry flavour, softened after chilling, goes very well with the apples.

SERVES 6

15 g / ½ oz butter
1 medium onion, diced
1 level tbsp curry powder
900 ml / 1½ pts light chicken stock
900 g / 2 lb dessert apples, peeled, cored and chopped
salt and pepper
juice of 1 lemon
150 ml / ¼ pt single cream
a few leaves of mint, chopped

Melt the butter, soften the onion and stir in the curry powder. Add the stock, the apples and a generous seasoning of salt and pepper. Bring to the boil, cover, turn down the heat and simmer for 45–60 minutes. Purée, strain through a sieve and cool. Add the lemon juice and cream when cold. Serve garnished with chopped mint.

CORIANDER SOUP

A garlicky onion and potato purée is chilled and laced with masses of finely chopped coriander. A hint of fire is added with cayenne pepper.

SERVES 6–8

4 tbsp olive oil
4 medium onions, coarsely chopped
2 large cloves of garlic, peeled and minced
4 medium potatoes, peeled and coarsely chopped
1.75 litres/3 pts chicken stock
salt
¼ tsp cayenne pepper
leaves from 1 large bunch of coriander, coarsely
   chopped

Heat 3 tbsp of olive oil and gently sauté the onions and garlic for about 5 minutes. Add the rest of the oil and the potatoes, and stir-fry for 60 seconds. Add the stock, bring to the boil, cover, and simmer for 15 minutes or until the potatoes are mushy. Purée until smooth, or force through a fine sieve. Pour the soup into a large bowl, salt to taste, and stir in the cayenne and coriander. Cover and refrigerate for 24 hours. Serve with good crusty bread.

GAZPACHO ANDALUZ

Gazpacho, a cold soup from Andalusia, is really a salad soup to be served on hot summer days and made with whatever is ripe and to hand. It generally includes tomatoes, cucumber, peppers, garlic and onion, all chopped very finely or blended to a pulp with bread, water, olive oil and vinegar. There are no exact proportions of ingredients of what is puréed and what isn't. Usually the soup is served iced, with ice-cubes, with a selection of other chopped garnishes to be added at the table. It is a dish to be played around with.

SERVES 6–8

900 g/2 lb ripe tomatoes, peeled and chopped
225 g/8 oz good breadcrumbs
1 medium cucumber, peeled, de-seeded and chopped
3 cloves of garlic, chopped
2 red peppers, cored, de-seeded and chopped
5 tbsp red or white wine vinegar
5 tbsp olive oil
1 tbsp tomato concentrate
salt and pepper
570 ml/1 pt iced water

Garnishes:

small croûtons fried in olive oil
hard-boiled eggs, whites chopped, yolks crumbled
spring onions, sliced
black olives
cucumber, peeled and diced
red or yellow pepper, diced

Mix together the tomatoes, breadcrumbs, cucumber, garlic, peppers, vinegar, olive oil and tomato concentrate in a large bowl. Season generously with salt and pepper. Liquidize in batches with a proportion of the water, then press through a sieve to a second bowl to remove any pips and skin. Chill for at least 4 hours. Set out some or all of the garnishes in little bowls for people to help themselves.

HUNGARIAN CHERRY SOUP

There are many variations of *meggyleves*, the famous sour cherry soup, but none to equal this one, which has been served for years at the Gay Hussar in Soho and was devised by its original owner, Victor Sassie. If you are unable to find wild sour cherries or morellos, use ordinary cherries, crack some of the cherry stones, simmer them gently in a little red wine and strain this liquid into the soup.

450 g/1 lb morello cherries
50 g/2 oz granulated sugar
1 bottle Riesling
a pinch of ground cinnamon
grated zest of 1 lemon
juice of 2 lemons
1 double measure of brandy
600 ml/1 pt soured cream

Stone the cherries over a pan so that none of the juice is lost. Put the stones and stalks into a pan with the sugar and wine. Bring to the boil and simmer for 5 minutes. Strain the liquid into a clean pan. Add the cinnamon, and the zest and juice of the lemons. Bring to the boil and tip in the cherries and all their juices (a rubber spatula is essential here). Bring back to the boil then remove immediately from the heat. Cool slightly and stir in the brandy.

Pour the soured cream into a large bowl. Slowly whisk in the soup, holding back the cherries for the moment, a little at a time, until the two mixtures have merged nicely. Tip in the rest of the fruit, stir thoroughly and chill for 3–4 hours before serving.

ICED CUCUMBER AND YOGHURT SOUP

This is a refreshing, delicious combination popular in Eastern
Europe and the Middle East and served as a salad in India
(*raita*), Turkey (*cacik*), and Greece (*tzatziki*).

SERVES 6

> 2 small cucumbers
> 1 tsp salt
> 275 ml/½ pt plain yoghurt
> 275 ml/½ pt tomato juice
> 1 small clove of garlic, finely chopped
> 900 ml/1½ pts light chicken stock
> a small bunch of mint
> 275 ml/½ pt single cream
> 8 drops of Tabasco sauce

Peel, de-seed and chop the cucumbers. Sprinkle on the salt
and leave to drain for 30 minutes. Blend the yoghurt, tomato
juice, garlic, chicken stock and mint (reserving a few leaves for
garnish). Strain through a fine sieve. Wash the cucumber and
squeeze out the excess moisture in a clean tea-towel. Stir into
the strained soup along with the cream and Tabasco. Taste
and adjust the seasoning. Chill until very cold, and garnish
with the reserved mint finely chopped.

NORMANDY APPLE SOUP

For Normandy, read cream and Calvados – a rich, thick and
alcoholic nectar.

SERVES 6

50 g / 2 oz butter
2 leeks, white part only, sliced
900 g / 2 lb dessert apples, peeled, cored and chopped
2 medium potatoes, peeled, chopped and rinsed
1.4 litres / 2½ pts light chicken stock
150 ml / ¼ pt double cream
2 tsp Calvados
a generous pinch of ground cinnamon
salt and pepper
2 whole dessert apples

Melt three-quarters of the butter and stir in the leeks. Cover
and sweat over a low heat for about 5 minutes. Add the apples
and cook, uncovered, for 5 minutes. Add the potatoes,
then the stock. Bring to the boil, then reduce the heat and
simmer, covered, for 45 minutes. Purée and strain through a
sieve. Stir in the cream, Calvados and cinnamon, taste and
season. Cool.

Just before serving, peel, core and dice the two whole apples.
Melt the rest of the butter and gently sauté the apples for about
5 minutes, until the outsides colour and the flesh is soft. Drain

carefully on absorbent paper. Garnish the chilled soup with the diced apple and serve.

PEAR AND WATERCRESS SOUP

The success of this soup relies on using sweet, ripe pears; their honeyed flesh is a delicious contrast with the peppery watercress. The cream is optional; it makes the soup very rich.

SERVES 4–6

3 large bunches of watercress
900 ml/ 1 ½ pts light chicken stock
4 ripe pears, cored, peeled and sliced
salt and pepper
juice of ½ a lemon
100 ml/ 4 fl oz double cream (optional)

Trim away the watercress stalks and bring them quickly to the boil in a pan with the stock, the pears, a generous pinch of salt and a few grinds of black pepper. Turn down the heat, cover, and simmer very gently for 15 minutes. Process in small batches with some watercress leaves in each batch. Pass through a fine sieve to catch the fibrous debris. Stir in the lemon juice, taste and adjust the seasoning. Cool, stir in the cream and chill for at least four hours.

WHITE GAZPACHO

White bread, almonds, water, olive oil, salt, garlic and white grapes don't sound very promising ingredients for a chilled summer soup. The combination goes back over 1,000 years, to the days when the Moors ruled much of Spain, and the soup's official name is *ajo blanco con uvas*. It has a surprisingly creamy texture with a sharp pungent flavour that is perfectly balanced by the sweet white grapes.

SERVES 6

225 g/8 oz stale white bread, crusts removed
900 ml/1½ pts iced water
110 g/4 oz almonds, peeled
3 large garlic cloves
2 tsp salt
6 tbsp olive oil
3 tbsp white wine or sherry vinegar
225 g/8 oz white grapes, split in half, de-pipped

Tear the bread into pieces and leave to soak in the iced water. Meanwhile place the almonds, garlic and salt in the bowl of a food processor. Process until the almonds are very finely ground. Use your hands to squeeze most of the liquid out of the bread and, with the motor running, add the bread to the almond mixture. Still with the motor running, pour the oil in a thin stream, then add the vinegar, followed by the rest of the water. Transfer the soup to a large china or glass bowl and add the grapes. Cover the soup with clingfilm and refrigerate for 4 hours before serving.

ISABEL ALLENDE · *Voices in My Ear*
NICHOLSON BAKER · *Playing Trombone*
LINDSEY BAREHAM · *The Little Book of Big Soups*
KAREN BLIXEN · *From the Ngong Hills*
DIRK BOGARDE · *Coming of Age*
ANTHONY BURGESS · *Childhood*
ANGELA CARTER · *Lizzie Borden*
CARLOS CASTANEDA · *The Sorcerer's Ring of Power*
ELIZABETH DAVID · *Peperonata and Other Italian Dishes*
RICHARD DAWKINS · *The Pocket Watchmaker*
GERALD DURRELL · *The Pageant of Fireflies*
RICHARD ELLMANN · *The Trial of Oscar Wilde*
EPICURUS · *Letter on Happiness*
MARIANNE FAITHFULL · *Year One*
KEITH FLOYD · *Hot and Spicy Floyd*
ALEXANDER FRATER · *Where the Dawn Comes Up Like Thunder*
ESTHER FREUD · *Meeting Bilal*
JOHN KENNETH GALBRAITH · *The Culture of Contentment*
ROB GRANT AND DOUG NAYLOR · *Scenes from the Dwarf*
ROBERT GRAVES · *The Gods of Olympus*
JANE GRIGSON · *Puddings*
SOPHIE GRIGSON · *From Sophie's Table*
KATHARINE HEPBURN · *Little Me*
SUSAN HILL · *The Badness Within Him*
ALAN HOLLINGHURST · *Adventures Underground*
BARRY HUMPHRIES · *Less is More Please*
HOWARD JACOBSON · *Expulsion from Paradise*
P. D. JAMES · *The Girl Who Loved Graveyards*
STEPHEN KING · *Umney's Last Case*
LAO TZU · *Tao Te Ching*
DAVID LEAVITT · *Chips Is Here*

PENGUIN 60s

LAURIE LEE · *To War in Spain*
PATRICK LEIGH FERMOR · *Loose as the Wind*
ELMORE LEONARD · *Trouble at Rindo's Station*
DAVID LODGE · *Surprised by Summer*
BERNARD MAC LAVERTY · *The Miraculous Candidate*
SHENA MACKAY · *Cloud-Cuckoo-Land*
NORMAN MAILER · *The Dressing Room*
PETER MAYLE · *Postcards from Summer*
JAN MORRIS · *Scenes from Havian Life*
BLAKE MORRISON · *Camp Cuba*
VLADIMIR NABOKOV · *Now Remember*
REDMOND O'HANLON · *A River in Borneo*
STEVEN PINKER · *Thinking in Tongues*
CRAIG RAINE · *Private View*
CLAUDIA RODEN · *Ful Medames and Other Vegetarian Dishes*
HELGE RUBINSTEIN · *Chocolate Parfait*
SIMON SCHAMA · *The Taking of the Bastille*
WILL SELF · *The Rock of Crack As Big As the Ritz*
MARK SHAND · *Elephant Tales*
NIGEL SLATER · *30-Minute Suppers*
RICK STEIN · *Fresh from the Sea*
LYTTON STRACHEY · *Florence Nightingale*
PAUL THEROUX · *Slow Trains to Simla*
COLIN THUBRON · *Samarkand*
MARK TULLY · *Beyond Purdah*
LAURENS VAN DER POST · *Merry Christmas, Mr Lawrence*
MARGARET VISSER · *More than Meets the Eye*
GAVIN YOUNG · *Something of Samoa*

and

Thirty Obituaries from Wisden · SELECTED BY MATTHEW ENGEL

READ MORE IN PENGUIN

For complete information about books available from Penguin and how to order them, please write to us at the appropriate address below. Please note that for copyright reasons the selection of books varies from country to country.

IN THE UNITED KINGDOM: Please write to *Dept. EP, Penguin Books Ltd, Bath Road, Harmondsworth, Middlesex UB7 0DA.*

IN THE UNITED STATES: Please write to *Consumer Sales, Penguin USA, P.O. Box 999, Dept. 17109, Bergenfield, New Jersey 07621-0120.* VISA and MasterCard holders call 1-800-253-6476 to order Penguin titles.

IN CANADA: Please write to *Penguin Books Canada Ltd, 10 Alcorn Avenue, Suite 300, Toronto, Ontario M4V 3B2.*

IN AUSTRALIA: Please write to *Penguin Books Australia Ltd, P.O. Box 257, Ringwood, Victoria 3134.*

IN NEW ZEALAND: Please write to *Penguin Books (NZ) Ltd, Private Bag 102902, North Shore Mail Centre, Auckland 10.*

IN INDIA: Please write to *Penguin Books India Pvt Ltd, 706 Eros Apartments, 56 Nehru Place, New Delhi 110 019.*

IN THE NETHERLANDS: Please write to *Penguin Books Netherlands bv, Postbus 3507, NL-1001 AH Amsterdam.*

IN GERMANY: Please write to *Penguin Books Deutschland GmbH, Metzlerstrasse 26, 60594 Frankfurt am Main.*

IN SPAIN: Please write to *Penguin Books S. A., Bravo Murillo 19, 1º B, 28015 Madrid.*

IN ITALY: Please write to *Penguin Italia s.r.l., Via Felice Casati 20, I-20124 Milano.*

IN FRANCE: Please write to *Penguin France S. A., 17 rue Lejeune, F-31000 Toulouse.*

IN JAPAN: Please write to *Penguin Books Japan, Ishikiribashi Building, 2-5-4, Suido, Bunkyo-ku, Tokyo 112.*

IN GREECE: Please write to *Penguin Hellas Ltd, Dimocritou 3, GR-106 71 Athens.*

IN SOUTH AFRICA: Please write to *Longman Penguin Southern Africa (Pty) Ltd, Private Bag X08, Bertsham 2013.*